LOOK!

Body Language in Art

LOOK!

Body Language in Art

Gillian Wolfe

FRANCES LINCOLN CHILDREN'S BOOKS

With thanks to Simon and Cherie Bakewell for *House on the Shore* inspiration, and Theodore Bakewell, aged 9, for his thoughts on *John Brown*.

PHOTOGRAPHIC ACKNOWLEDGMENTS

For permission to reproduce the paintings on the following pages and for supplying photographs, the Publishers would like to thank:

The Art Institute of Chicago: 31 (All Rights reserved by The Art Institute of Chicago and VAGA, New York, NY, 1930.934)
Bildarchiv Foto Marburg: 19
Bridgeman Art Library: 1, 2–3, 8–9, 16–17 (© Estate of Mark Gertler), 22–23, 26–27, 32–33
Dulwich Picture Gallery, London: 6, 18
© The Solomon R. Guggenheim Foundation, New York: 24 (© ADAGP, Paris and DACS, London 2004)
Photo © 1982 The Metropolitan Museum of Art: Cover and 28–29
Photo © 1977 The Metropolitan Museum of Art: 21 (© Estate of John Steuart Curry)
Norman Rockwell Museum: 35 (printed by permission of the Norman Rockwell Family Agency, © 1947 the Norman Rockwell Family Entities)
© Peter Stanick: 12
The Royal Collection © 2004, Her Majesty Queen Elizabeth II: 14–15 (photographer Rodney Todd-White)
© Tate, London (2004): 7 (© Succession Picasso/DACS 2004)
V&A Picture Library: 10–11

First published in Great Britain in 2004 by
Frances Lincoln Children's Books, 4 Torriano Mews,
Torriano Avenue, London NW5 2RZ

www.franceslincoln.com

Distributed in the USA by Publishers Group West

British Library Cataloguing in Publication Data available on request

ISBN 1-84507-034-8

Printed in Singapore

1 3 5 7 9 8 6 4 2

Contents

Look at Faces   6

Look at Hands   14

Look at Body Pose   20

Look for the Message   28

Look It Up   36

Index   40

Faces and Feelings

Carlo Dolci, *St Catherine of Siena*

St Catherine's gentle face is calm and still and yet her expression shows you that she is quietly suffering a great sadness.

As a nun she has devoted herself to a life of prayer. She is painted here wearing a crown of thorns in memory of Jesus who was made to wear one before he died. She is grieving for the way he suffered.

Do you feel that you can almost touch the tear that rolls down her cheek? Even without the tear, can you still tell that she is feeling sad?

★ Draw a gentle face with curving lines and soft colours. Then draw a furious face with jagged shapes, hard lines and angry colours.

Pablo Picasso, *Weeping Woman*

Have you noticed that when people are desperately upset their faces seem to crumple into strange shapes?

Picasso shows us the face of a woman who is suffering a terrible sadness. Jagged shapes express her feelings of sorrow, anger and despair.

The woman is savagely biting her handkerchief in her misery.

Can you decide which shapes are fingers and which are tears in the confusion?

Look at the clashing colours! These are deliberately harsh and bright to show how much the woman is suffering.

Terrified

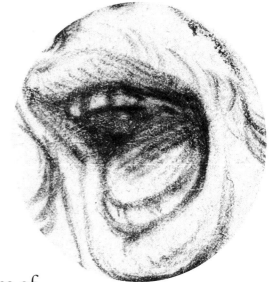

Look at those wide, staring eyes. Look at the mouth open in a cry or a scream, and the wild flowing hair. What are the emotions shown in this man's face? Is he furiously angry, terrified out of his wits, or surprised by an enemy attack?

This artist made hundreds of sketches of people's faces. This one represents terror. He then used the sketches when creating his paintings to make his characters' expressions look as real as possible. Even the short stabbing pencil marks for shading the face add to the feeling of alarm.

This artist wants you to understand exactly what his people are feeling.

★ Ask a friend to make a really ferocious face expression and try to draw it. You will probably both end up laughing so try and draw that too!

Charles Le Brun, *Terror*

Effroy. 7

8

Angry or not?

What does this man's face say about his feelings?
Is the face frightening? Is it funny?

This man is an actor. In Japanese theatre the actor is expected to exaggerate all his expressions and actions. Some plays are very complicated. When the actors exaggerate everything, people can understand the plot more easily. Just look at his downturned

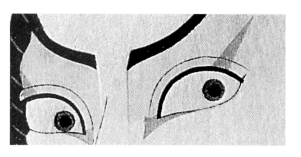

mouth, the frowning eyebrows and the staring black eye-dots.

This face of a fierce Japanese warrior has been painted on a fan as a decoration.

★ For a few fun minutes, look at yourself in a mirror and see how many amazing face expressions you can make.

Keeping your body and face quite still, can you use your eyes alone to show the way you feel?

Shunkosai Hokushu, *The Kabuki actor Nakamura Utaemon III in the Role of a Samurai*

Peter Stanick, *Dead Shark*

Shocked!

Have you seen something like this picture in comic books? The artist has deliberately made his painting look like a cartoon.

Do you think these faces look like real people? Are eyes or mouths really like this? The artist cleverly catches your attention with his bold and inventive shapes.

This artist has added words under the picture that make fun of art. Two people gaze at what they expect to be a beautiful piece of artwork. When they realise that it is actually a dead fish, they say in horror, 'That's art? It's just a dead shark!'

They are completely shocked and their faces show it.

★ Make a comic strip to tell a story. Exaggerate the face expressions to get your message over. Why not add speech bubbles?

With a friend, each of you draw five faces and give every one a different expression. Swap papers and try to guess what the expressions mean.

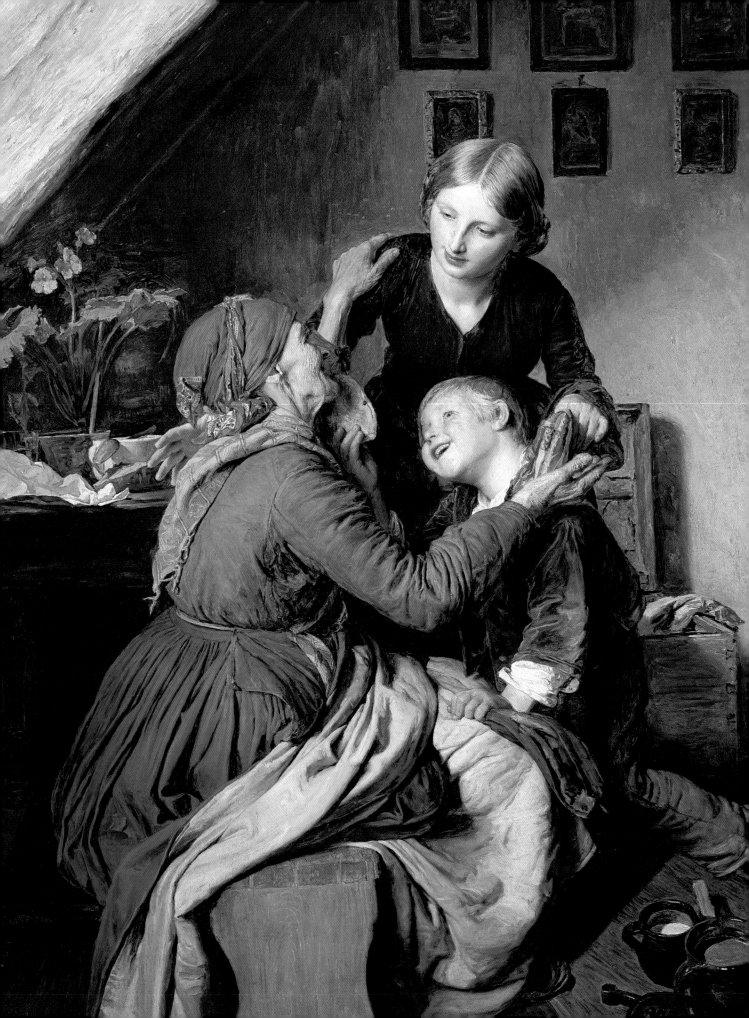

Happy Birthday

How many hands and arms can you see in this picture? They are all wrapped around in a birthday hug for Grandmother.

Can you see how the hand gestures link everyone together, the mother, child and Grandma? The hands are important: they hold the three people in a close family circle. The boy watches Grandmother's eyes as he holds up his own gift. Has she noticed his present?

Did you know that this painting of a birthday celebration was actually given to Queen Victoria, by her beloved husband Prince Albert, on her own birthday? They both liked scenes showing the joys of family life, perhaps because they themselves had such a big family.

★ Compare your hands with those of an older person. How do they differ in shape, colour and texture? Which is the more interesting to draw?

Ferdinand Georg Waldmüller, *The Grandmother's Birthday*

Tender Touch

With just one glance at this picture you can understand straight away what the artist wants to tell you.

The grandfather is a Jewish Rabbi, or teacher. He tenderly touches his grandchild's chin, as if he wants to show her off to us. You can see that he loves her and is proud of her.

His big, sad eyes also look thoughtful. As well as being a proud grandfather, perhaps he is also wishing that he were young again.

Without the delicate hand gesture would you have known about the loving feelings between the two?

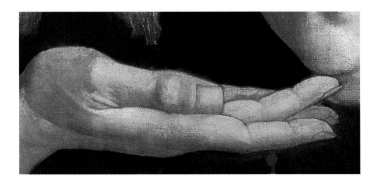

★ Act out a scene using your hands but not using any words at all. Can you still be understood?

Mark Gertler, *The Rabbi and his Grandchild*

Tough Guy

A follower of Jusepe de Ribera, *The Locksmith*

O ut of the darkness looms the figure of a man who makes and mends locks. His face is half-hidden in deep shadow. Is he listening to someone? Is his arm raised because he wants to hide something? His elbow almost seems to be pushing us out of the way to stop us watching what his hands are up to.

What is he doing? His hands are turning a key. Is he mending the lock?

Does he seem more like a thief than an honest tradesman? Would you trust this man?

★ Try to draw hands making all sorts of gestures. Why not use your own hand as a model?

Promises

What are they doing that seems to absorb them so much?

In one hand the woman delicately holds a wild rose to show us that she is in love. In her other hand she holds a wide gold band. It is actually a ring to hold together the tassel on the man's cap, which rests on his shoulder. Why should she hold tightly to his cap strings? Is she telling us that he belongs to her?

The floating banner explains that the gold band is a vow of faithfulness.

Master of the Housebook, *The Betrothal*

Action Man

Danger! The powerful body of a huge man almost bursts out of the picture as if he is coming towards you to shout a desperate warning. Something awful has happened. The man almost looks as if he has suffered an electric shock! Every nerve of his body is on red alert.

Look behind him. In the distance, on one side of him, a raging tornado spirals to the sky while on the other side a blazing fire rips across the land.

Kansas is a hot, dry mid-west state in America where life was hard for the early settlers. Nature can be cruel, sending gales, storms, fire and drought that destroy all the hard work and effort that goes into sowing crops and building homes.

Only the strongest can survive. John Brown, a giant-sized figure, is ready to cope with the worst that nature can bring.

★ Pretend a wild animal, perhaps a lion, is about to pounce on you – how would your body shape change if you were in a really dangerous situation? Try to capture the pose in a sketch.

John Steuart Curry, *John Brown*

Best Friends

Dogs have a special closeness to people. Look at this one in the painting. It leans against the little girl with its head on her shoulder as if to say, 'Never mind, I'm your friend anyway!' It is trying to comfort her. Animals are brilliant at letting us know how they feel.

The little girl is sitting on the stairs, looking very sorry for herself. Is she trying to put off going to bed to the last minute, hoping not to be noticed behind the banister? Is she listening to whatever is going on downstairs and wishing she were part of it? Is she feeling cross and unfairly treated?

However she feels, her faithful dog is there for her.

The young girl is actually the artist's own daughter with the family dog. Her father has perfectly captured the sympathy between the two.

How does an animal look when it is hot and tired, friendly, alarmed, or angry? Try some sketches.

23

iton Riviere, *Sympathy*

Look at Body Pose

Ready to Win

His head is down, and his body hunched forward over the handlebars of his bike. This cyclist is straining every muscle.

Determined to be first past the post, he puts every last bit of effort into winning the race.

Over his shoulder he is aware of another cyclist very near him. Can you see the way the artist has shown one of the bike wheels spinning, to give the impression of speed?

The artist has made the cyclist's body transparent so that it seems as if he is whizzing by so fast that he hardly gets in the way of our view.

Through his face we can see the watching and cheering crowds. Do you think they are in the cyclist's mind as he races, or is he concentrating on the finishing-line ahead?

★ The cyclist's body is like a jigsaw of printed and collaged shapes slotting in together. Cut out shapes like these and stick them together to see if you can create an action-packed pose.

Jean Metzinger, *At The Cycle-Race Track*

Look at Body Pose

Ready to Drop

From a cloudless blue sky, the fierce midday sun beats down on the golden cornfields. The two harvesters are worn out after hours of hot, dusty work. They probably began at dawn and now need a well-earned rest. In the shadow of a haystack they throw down their scythes or cutting tools. The man has slipped off his shoes. They sink on to a cushion of straw and let their exhausted bodies give in to a welcome doze.

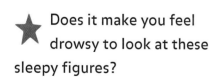

Van Gogh paints with rippling brush strokes. His people seem to merge in with the landscape, almost as if they are a part of the loose hay around them.

★ Does it make you feel drowsy to look at these sleepy figures?

How would you describe the pose of the man and woman?

Try to sketch these body poses:
• relaxed at home
• fed up and miserable
• defiant and cross
• feeling ill
• feeling energetic

Vincent van Gogh, *Noon, Rest from Work*

Georges de La Tour, *The Fortune Teller*

Look for the Message

Crafty Crooks

How has the artist let you know that something strange is going on in this picture? Can you make a guess at what is happening?

This is a young and trusting man. You can see by his clothes that he is quite wealthy and this has attracted the attention of a weird-looking group of people.

The old woman is a fortune teller and the young man has paid her a large silver coin. While he gives her all his attention, the other people have their own plans. Just look at those dodgy expressions! Can you see what they are doing?

⭐ How would you finish this story? Write your own ending or draw a picture of what you think happened next.

Does this scene make you feel worried about the fate of the young man? Will he realise in time that he is being tricked?

Look for the Message

No Nonsense

It is not only dramatic poses which give us messages about people.

Do you think that this man's expression is stern and solemn? What about the woman, whose eyes look away from us?

The man looks as if he knows all about hard work. His strong hand tightly grips a sharp pitchfork, as if he has just been making hay. She stands stiffly by his side. What is she thinking about? We wonder what life was like for people in mid-west America where farmers had to be strong and independent to survive.

Although these two are standing close, there is no feeling of togetherness. His 'no nonsense' direct gaze does not welcome us into their world. They stand like a wall between us and the farm behind, as if protecting it from strangers. Even the neat house with its church-like window and drawn blinds appears closed and private.

★ Strong vertical lines all over the picture reinforce the stiff body pose of the couple. How many vertical lines can you count in this calm yet powerful picture? How does this picture make you feel?

Grant Wood, *American Gothic*

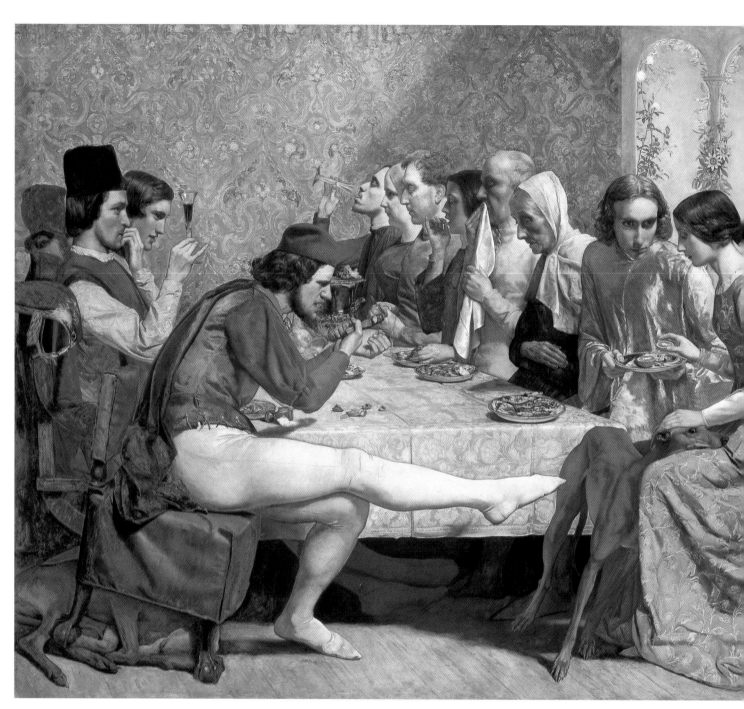

Sir John Everett Millais, *Lorenzo and Isabella*

Plotting!

This is a picture of love and hate. Lorenzo loves Isabella. He gazes intently at her while offering her an orange. She delicately takes a piece of fruit whilst stroking the head of her devoted dog.

These two don't seem to notice that across the table Isabella's brothers are burning with fury. The brothers are outraged that the poor and humble Lorenzo should dare to love their sister. She is expected to marry a rich and powerful man.

The brother at the front glares fiercely while his body leans forward aggressively. He grips a nutcracker in a clenched fist as if it were a weapon he would very much like to use.

Most terrible of all is his long powerful leg. It stretches right across the picture and viciously kicks out at Isabella's gentle greyhound.

We can guess whom he really wants to kick!

★ Draw a family picture to show how each person is feeling about the others.

Look for the Message

Family Life

One bright sunny morning a family sets off for an outing to Lake Bennington in Vermont, America. In the car are Mum, Dad, four children, Grandma and the family dog.

Look at the top half of the picture. As the car glides through the countryside, everyone is eager and alert, looking forward to a fun day. Now look at the bottom half of the picture. In the evening, a different-looking family returns to a darkening city.

Look at the changes in the 'before' picture of the family going out and the 'after' picture of the family coming home. Which person looks the most exhausted? Who looks the most harassed? Is there anyone who is unchanged?

How have the face expressions, hand gestures and the body shapes altered? Look at the hair ribbon, the bubble gum and Dad's hat and cigar. Just look at the dog – its body language says it all!

Can you remember a family outing like this? Draw a picture of it and add comments from your family about their memories of the day.

Look again at the driver. It is in fact Norman Rockwell. The artist has painted himself into the picture. Why not paint yourself into yours too?

Norman Rockwell, *Going and Coming*

Look It Up

Here you can find out more about the art and artists in this book, including when the paintings were made, when the artists lived, and where you can see the paintings.

Page 6
St Catherine of Siena, *c.* 1665–70
Carlo Dolci (1616–86)
Dulwich Picture Gallery, London

Some artists are gifted even as children. Dolci was only sixteen when he painted one of his most famous portraits. He was the leading painter in Florence, a town in Italy where the arts flourished. Despite his success, he was always haunted with self-doubt about his talents.

Dolci's painting style was extremely detailed. His paintings are usually very small, and are often of religious subjects. Each painting took a long time to complete. A fellow artist said that Dolci spent so much time in finishing his work he would starve!

Page 7
Weeping Woman, 1937
Pablo Picasso (1881–1973)
Tate Collection

Picasso, a Spanish artist, was a genius. He learned to draw before he could talk and his first word was *lapis* (pencil). He disliked school and worked at nothing but art. As his extraordinary talents developed he moved away from the rules of traditional painting. His painting style changed many times. To many people, 'modern art' means the work of Picasso. He made drawings, paintings, collages, prints, theatre sets, sculptures, pottery and ceramics. He is probably best known for his Cubist pictures which use geometric shapes.

Pages 8–9
Terror, 1663
Charles Le Brun (1619–90)
The Louvre, Paris

Le Brun made up very strict rules and regulations about painting, which influenced French artists for many years. He also wrote exact directions about how best to express emotions and passions in painting.

Le Brun was almost totally in charge of the arts in France under King Louis XIV and was as much a clever politician as an artist. A successful and powerful man, he made many paintings and over 2000 of his drawings are in the Louvre in Paris.

Pages 10–11
The Kabuki actor Nakumura Utaemon III in the Role of a Samurai
from the series *Famous Roles of Utaemon*, 1825
Shunkosai Hokushu (working 1808–32)
Victoria and Albert Museum, London

We know very little about this Japanese artist. We do know that Hokushu owned a paper store in Osaka, and that he was considered to be the best printmaker in the region.

He had a reputation for fine art prints of scenes from Japanese plays, and he is thought to be the founder of the Osaka school of actor portraiture. Hokushu was probably a pupil of the most famous Japanese printmaker, Hohusai, best known for his series of 36 views of Mount Fuji and more than 30,000 prints.

Page 12
Dead Shark, 1997
Peter Stanick, (born 1953)
Private Collection

Bold cartoon-like techniques quickly get this artist's message across. Peter Stanick is an American painter with a sense of humour about art and artists. He likes to make fun of the over-serious way that people think about art.

His shapes and lines are simple yet powerful. His strong colours shout. He uses words as part of his pictures, making them look as if they are part of a comic strip. The words make teasing comments which grab the attention of the viewer.

Pages 14–15
The Grandmother's Birthday, 1856
Ferdinand Georg Waldmüller (1793–1865)
Osborne House, Isle of Wight (on loan from The Royal Collection)

Waldmüller was an Austrian artist who painted portraits, landscapes and some tiny pictures called miniatures. He was also a teacher of painting and sometimes he upset the other teachers at his academy with his strong opinions.

He liked to paint ordinary country people in scenes showing the joys of family life. His painting style showed great attention to detail.

During a visit to London he sold 31 paintings to Queen Victoria, her husband Prince Albert and their friends.

Pages 16–17
The Rabbi and his Grandchild, 1913
Mark Gertler (1891–1939)
Southampton City Art Gallery

One day, when he was 14, Gertler found a book about a famous artist in a second-hand bookshop. This was his first knowledge of art. He began art classes but could not afford to keep going so he became an apprentice in a firm of glass painters.

A prize in a national art competition led him to art school. Here he met talented, fashionable and famous people. Despite this, his paintings showed the extreme hardship of his childhood as the son of Jewish refugees from Poland.

Page 18
The Locksmith, *c.* 1630
A follower of Jusepe de Ribera (1591–1652)
Dulwich Picture Gallery, London

Ribera was a Spanish artist. As a young man he went to Italy and settled in the town of Naples. Ribera's own artwork was a blend of Spanish and Italian styles. He had an enormous influence on the other artists working in Naples at that time, whose painting style became like his. This style is called Neapolitan.

Ribera's paintings are realistic with strong light and dark contrasts. Sometimes his subjects are brutal, and even his religious or mythological scenes are forcefully painted.

Page 19
The Betrothal, *c.* 1484
Master of the Housebook (working *c.* 1470–1500)
Gotha Museum, Gotha

We do not know who the Master of the Housebook was. All we know is that he made a series of drawings and prints showing scenes of everyday life in a castle in the Rhine area of Germany. This series is called a Housebook.

We do know that the artist made about 90 prints, but we are not even sure whether he was German or Dutch. These days the artist is an important person but at the time of *The Betrothal*, the artist was thought of more as a master craftsman.

Page 21
John Brown, *c.* 1939
John Steuart Curry (1897–1946)
The Metropolitan Museum of Art, New York
(Arthur Hoppock Hearn Fund, 1950.50.94.1)

A farm boy from the state of Kansas, John Steuart Curry grew up to become a famous painter, but he never forgot the countryside of his boyhood. He painted the struggle of man against the harshness of nature that brought fierce heat, terrible storms and tornado winds.

Many of his paintings are of small-town life, people gathering to defend their farms, or crowds at circuses. He was the first artist to be employed by a university to inspire people in country areas to be more creative.

Pages 22–23
Sympathy, 1877
Briton Riviere (1840–1920)
Royal Holloway and Bedford New College, Surrey

Riviere had exhibited his work by the age of 12. His father, grandfather and great grandfather were all artists. A tireless worker, he painted by day and drew illustrations for magazines in the evening. This late-night work eventually damaged his eyes.

He became famous for being able to show the sympathy between animals and people. Animals often play the leading part in his pictures. When his portraits feature a man and a dog, the dog is often better painted than the man. Riviere was an extremely popular artist. This painting was one of the most requested reproductions of the Victorian age.

Page 24
At The Cycle-Race Track, *c.* 1914
Jean Metzinger (1883–1956)
The Solomon R. Guggenheim Foundation, New York,
Peggy Guggenheim Collection, Venice, 1976 (76.2553.18)

Metzinger was part of a group of artists called Cubists. These artists experimented with shapes in a new way. Metzinger wrote the first book about this style of painting. Cubist artists combined several different views of an object in one painting. They thought this had an advantage over a single view because it gave a more complete idea of the object.

There are different styles within Cubism. Metzinger used flat shapes and patterns, often with collage.

Pages 26–27
Noon, Rest from Work, 1890
Vincent van Gogh (1853–90)
Musée d'Orsay, Paris

For much of his short life, van Gogh was poor, depressed and ill. Yet despite this he has left the world hundreds of marvellous drawings and paintings, all made in the last 10 years of his life. He worked very fast, his excited brush strokes showing his energy and strong passions. Sadly his work was not liked in his lifetime, and he never knew that he would become one of the most famous artists of all time.

Pages 28–29 (and cover)
The Fortune Teller, probably 1630s
Georges de La Tour (1593–1652)
The Metropolitan Museum of Art, New York (Rogers Fund, 1960.60.30)

Very few pictures were painted by La Tour, only about forty in all. He lived with his family in a small French town far away from the artistic life of the city. For a long time the brilliance of his art was not understood. He developed a style of painting which simplified figures into almost geometric shapes in a calm composition. Yet he showed exactly how his people were feeling.

Two hundred and fifty years before the electric light bulb Georges de La Tour was fascinated by the light and shadow effect of candlelight on the subject.

Page 31
American Gothic, 1930
Grant Wood (1891–1942)
The Art Institute of Chicago (Friends of American Art Collection)

After studying wood and metalcraft, Grant Wood opened a handcraft shop in Iowa. His real love was painting so he studied art in Chicago and Europe. Whilst in Germany he discovered paintings of everyday scenes by Old Master artists. These influenced him so much that he changed his free style of painting to a more detailed style, like that of the Dutch painters he so admired. He won a bronze medal at the Institute of Chicago for his picture, *American Gothic*. Some people were upset at this portrayal of 'plain country folk'. Others thought that he summed up the spirit of survival in the American midwest very well in this famous picture.

Pages 32–33
Lorenzo and Isabella, 1849
Sir John Everett Millais (1829–96)
The Walker Art Gallery, Liverpool

A child who shows a brilliant talent at a very young age is called an 'infant prodigy'. Millais was one, entering art school at only 11 years old and already famous at 19. He was a gifted painter of portraits, history scenes, and scenes of everyday life. Millais and his friends formed an art movement called the Pre-Raphaelite Brotherhood that tried to be true to nature. Their pictures were painted on a white background for the greatest colour brilliance.

Page 35
Going and Coming, 1947
Norman Rockwell (1894–1978)
Norman Rockwell Museum, Stockbridge, Massachusetts

An American illustrator and painter, Norman Rockwell produced artwork continuously for over 60 years. During that time he provided a fascinating window into changes in American life during the 20th century. Rockwell's main work was as a magazine illustrator. He designed over 300 covers for the *Saturday Evening Post*. This took his artwork into the homes of millions of Americans. Most of his illustrations featured ordinary American people. His family, friends, neighbours and local townspeople were his models. His pictures always tell a story.

Index of Paintings and Artists

American Gothic 30–31
At The Cycle-Race Track 24–25
Betrothal, The 19
Brun, Charles Le 8–9
Catherine of Siena, St 6
Curry, John Steuart 20–21
Dead Shark 12–13
Dolci, Carlo 6
Fortune Teller, The 28–29
Gertler, Mark 16–17
Gogh, Vincent van 26–27
Going and Coming 34–35
Grandmother's Birthday, The 14–15
Hokushu, Shunkosai 10–11
John Brown 20–21
Kabuki actor Nakamura Utaemon III
*   in the Role of a Samurai, The* 10–11

Locksmith, The 18
Lorenzo and Isabella 32–33
Master of the Housebook 19
Metzinger, Jean 24–25
Millais, Sir John Everett 32–33
Noon, Rest from Work 26–27
Picasso, Pablo 7
Rabbi and his Grandchild, The 16–17
Ribera, Jusepe de 18
Riviere, Briton 22–23
Rockwell, Norman 34–35
Stanick, Peter 12–13
Sympathy 22–23
Terror 8–9
Tour, Georges de La 28–29
Waldmüller, Ferdinand Georg 14–15
Weeping Woman 7
Wood, Grant 30–31